NOT PLAYING
by the RULES

21 Female Athletes Who Changed Sports

Lesa Cline-Ransome

Alfred A. Knopf
New York

THIS IS A BORZOI BOOK PUBLISHED BY ALFRED A. KNOPF

Text copyright © 2020 by Lesa Cline-Ransome
Jacket photos clockwise from top left: Nadia Comăneci copyright © by Bettmann/Getty Images;
Serena Williams copyright © by Icon Sportswire/Chaz Niell/Getty Images; Mo'ne Davis copyright © by Rob Carr/Getty Images;
Mia Hamm copyright © by Timothy A. Clary/Getty Images

Photo credits:
Constance Applebee: PD-US; Lizzie Arlington: PD-US; Ethelda Bleibtrey: PD-US; Alice Coachman: Bettmann/Getty Images;
Nadia Comăneci: Bettmann/Getty Images; Mo'ne Davis: Rob Carr/Getty Images; Babe Didrikson Zaharias: Underwood Archives/Getty Images;
Gabby Douglas: Tim Clayton—Corbis/Getty Images; Bobbi Gibb: Fred Kaplan/Getty Images; Althea Gibson: Bettmann/Getty Images;
Diana Golden: Disabled Sports USA; Mia Hamm: David Madison/Getty Images; Flo Hyman: Richard Mackson/Getty Images;
Joy Johnson: Randi Lynn Beach; Lisa Leslie: Jesse D. Garrabrant/Getty Images; Nancy Lieberman: Barry Gossage/Getty Images;
Yusra Mardini: Mario Tama/Getty Images; Tatyana McFadden: Atsushi Tomura/Getty Images;
Ibtihaj Muhammad: Ezra Shaw/Getty Images; Venus and Serena Williams: Mitchell Gerber/Getty Images

Visit us on the Web! rhcbooks.com

Educators and librarians, for a variety of teaching tools, visit us at
RHTeachersLibrarians.com

Library of Congress Cataloging-in-Publication Data is available upon request.
ISBN 978-1-5247-6453-1 (trade) — ISBN 978-1-5247-6454-8 (lib. bdg.) — ISBN 978-1-5247-6455-5 (ebook)

The text of this book is set in 12-point Goudy Old Style.
Hand-lettering by Casey Moses

MANUFACTURED IN CHINA
April 2020
10 9 8 7 6 5 4 3 2 1

First Edition

In memory of Louise Stokes (October 27, 1913–March 25, 1978),
inspiration and fellow Maldonian.
The "Malden Meteor," who blazed a trail for all of us . . .

Being a member of a team gives you confidence and power.

This is the breath of life.

CONSTANCE APPLEBEE
Field Hockey
JUNE 4, 1873–JANUARY 26, 1981

WHEN CONSTANCE APPLEBEE BOOKED ROUND-TRIP PASSAGE from England to America in 1901 to take a summer course at Harvard University, she never imagined it would be decades before she used her return ticket. But then Constance, a graduate of the British College of Physical Education, discovered that musical chairs and drop the handkerchief were the main sports offered for female students at American colleges. She took a stand.

"We play those games at parties," she told her hosts. "For exercise, we play hockey." Gathering up makeshift supplies and willing volunteers, Constance demonstrated the sport she played in her home country. One guest, Vassar athletic director Harriet Ballintine, insisted she demonstrate the sport at her school. From 1901 to 1902, Constance traveled with her equipment from Vassar to Smith to Wellesley to Mount Holyoke to Radcliffe to Bryn Mawr to teach female college students the sport of field hockey and the importance of physical activity. With each school she visited, the popularity of field hockey began to spread to women on college campuses throughout the country.

In 1904, she was hired to coach Bryn Mawr's first field hockey team. As a coach, Constance demanded that her players exercise daily. Those who missed practice were required to pay a fine, which helped cover the cost of equipment, and she often shouted her signature insult from the sidelines: "Put your claws on your stick, you one-legged turnip!"

Instead of rebelling, her players adored her and insisted her methods made them stronger women. And it was Constance's hope that their newfound strength in sports would translate into strength in fighting for women's rights and in the voting booth.

In the 1920s, she founded the *Sportswoman*, the first magazine devoted entirely to women's athletics, and opened a field hockey camp in Mount Pocono, Pennsylvania, serving one thousand girls taught by the best players and coaches from around the world.

She retired from coaching in 1929 but continued to advise teams and coach her players informally, playing on the fields until she was ninety-seven years old.

She goes in to win every time.

LIZZIE ARLINGTON
Baseball
1876(?)–1917(?)

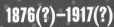

A WOMAN HAD TO BE STRONG if she wanted to play baseball in the 1800s. Bats weighed nearly three pounds, and a woman, clad in a heavy wool dress, had to hit the ball, drop the bat, drape her skirt over her arm, and run to first base. Most people agreed with major league pitcher Albert Spalding that baseball was just "too strenuous for womankind." But Lizzie Arlington was one woman who disagreed.

Lizzie didn't mind being the first. In the coal-mining town of Mahanoy City, Pennsylvania, Lizzie was the first girl to ride a bicycle. She loved to roller-skate. She competed in polo matches and was a pretty good shot with a rifle. Barely five feet tall and stocky, Lizzie didn't exactly look like a baseball player, but her father and brothers taught her to hit, catch, and slide. Another local, future major league player John Elmer Stivetts, taught her to pitch.

On July 2, 1898, over fifty years after baseball rules were established, Lizzie suited up in a gray uniform with a knee-length skirt and black stockings, her hair tucked in a cap. She stepped on the pitcher's mound for the Philadelphia Nationals reserve team as the first woman ever to sign a contract in the minor leagues, playing with all men.

Promoter William Conner became her manager, promising to pay her one hundred dollars per week. He hoped that a woman pitcher would draw thousands to the ball field, but when only five hundred showed, he cut Lizzie loose. Three days later, Lizzie signed herself for a second pitching spot with another minor league team, the Reading Coal Barons, and pitched a scoreless ninth inning. "Good for Lizzie!" shouted the one thousand fans who bought tickets, two hundred of them women.

Lizzie began barnstorming—traveling all over the country—with the all-female Bloomer Girls teams. "She is a success," one sports reporter wrote, "for a woman."

Swimming is the best sport in the world for women.

ETHELDA BLEIBTREY
Swimming
FEBRUARY 27, 1902–MAY 6, 1978

BY THE TIME THE POLICE ARRIVED at Brooklyn's Manhattan Beach, Ethelda was already waist-deep in the water. Handcuffed and led off to jail, seventeen-year-old Ethelda was charged with a criminal offense—removing her stockings to swim.

Since her very first dip in Saratoga Lake, little Ethelda loved the water. But her parents worried about her. She was sixteen when polio left her spine curved and her body weak. Her doctor suggested she start swimming to help her regain strength. She kept swimming to spend time in the water with her best friend, Charlotte Boyle. Ethelda not only got stronger, she got faster, leaving Charlotte behind time and again. When they swam at Manhattan Beach and the heavy wool from Ethelda's swimsuit slowed her down, she peeled off her stockings, resulting in her arrest.

Ethelda continued to spend most of her time in water. She swam so hard and fast, she became the top swimmer in each of her amateur meets and caught the eye of coach Louis de Breda Handley, a former Olympian. He agreed to train her, and she won every race she swam. After only one year of competing, Ethelda raced Australian Olympic gold medalist Fanny Durack during her U.S. tour. She was the first woman to beat the champion. Coach Handley knew Ethelda was ready for deeper waters.

The only Olympic events for women in 1920 were tennis, diving, and swimming. Of the more than twenty-six hundred Olympians at the Summer Games in Antwerp, Belgium, sixty-three were women. Of these, twelve were Americans, and six of those twelve were on the swim team. With her best friend and fellow Olympic swimmer, Charlotte, by her side, Ethelda and the rest of the women's swim team boarded a ship bound for Belgium.

The swimmers raced in estuaries with water so cold, they sprinted to the locker rooms to warm up after each finish. By the time the games ended, Ethelda had won three gold medals and set three world records. She was the first U.S. Olympian to win three golds and the only person ever to win all of the women's swimming events. Still, Ethelda was disappointed. She could have won four gold medals, she said, "but they didn't have women's backstroke."

MILDRED ELLA "BABE" DIDRIKSON ZAHARIAS
golf
JUNE 26, 1911–SEPTEMBER 27, 1956

IN THE EARLY-MORNING HOURS OF JUNE 26, 1911, an explosion on a barge reverberated through Hannah and Ole Didrikson's neighborhood in Port Arthur, Texas, setting much of the town ablaze. Minutes later, their red-faced baby, Mildred Ella, hurried into the world.

Little Mildred caused a ruckus wherever she went. She lit matches between her siblings' toes and beat up anyone who teased her. In school, she was told she was "too good to play with girls" and was put on boys' sports teams. When she hit five home runs in one baseball game, she earned the nickname "Babe," after major leaguer Babe Ruth.

"I came out here to beat everybody in sight, and that is what I am going to do," she told her rivals before she competed in track and field, tennis, diving, bowling, and even billiards. After she joined her high school basketball team, the team went undefeated.

To help support her family, Babe accepted a job as a secretary for an insurance company that needed her talents on their company basketball team. She led the Golden Cyclones to the national championship for three straight years. In the off-season, her coach kept her busy with track-and-field events, and in 1931, she competed as the only member of her company track team at the National Women's Amateur Athletic Union track meet. She single-handedly captured the championship title by winning first place in seven of the ten sporting events. And she scored second in an eighth. The next year, at age twenty-one, she qualified for the U.S. Olympic track team and won two gold medals and one silver, setting new world records in the javelin, 80-meter hurdles, and the high jump.

When asked by a reporter "Is there *anything* you don't play?" Babe replied, "Yeah, dolls."

After watching golfing great Bobby Jones during an exhibition, Babe decided she would experiment with the only sport she hadn't tried. She practiced six days a week, sometimes sixteen hours a day, hitting fifteen hundred balls daily until her hands were bloodied and callused. Finally, she was ready to compete. Losing didn't come easy to Babe, so after being narrowly defeated in her first amateur tournament in 1934, she won the next seventeen. She entered to compete in the 1938 Los Angeles Open, an all-male event.

Never afraid to tout her talents, Babe would ask at the start of tournaments, "Okay, Babe's here! Now, who's gonna finish second?"

I've always believed I could do whatever I set my mind to do.

ALICE COACHMAN
Track and Field

NOVEMBER 9, 1923–JULY 14, 2014

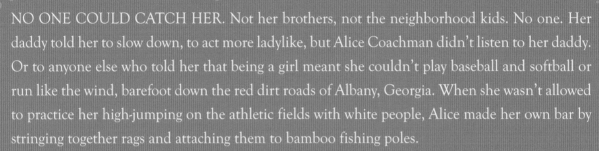

NO ONE COULD CATCH HER. Not her brothers, not the neighborhood kids. No one. Her daddy told her to slow down, to act more ladylike, but Alice Coachman didn't listen to her daddy. Or to anyone else who told her that being a girl meant she couldn't play baseball and softball or run like the wind, barefoot down the red dirt roads of Albany, Georgia. When she wasn't allowed to practice her high-jumping on the athletic fields with white people, Alice made her own bar by stringing together rags and attaching them to bamboo fishing poles.

Fred and Evelyn Coachman had ten children and they didn't have time for a daughter who misbehaved, danced, and played sports when there was work to be done. But a teacher and an aunt, who both knew of Alice's talent for sports, told her to keep right on competing. Alice showed everyone on her high school track-and-field team that you didn't need shoes to break records, when she earned herself a full scholarship to Tuskegee Institute. But free tuition meant that when Alice wasn't practicing, studying, or winning national championships in the 100-meter dash, 4 × 100 relay, and high jump, she had to earn her keep by maintaining the tennis courts, sewing football uniforms, and cleaning the gym.

Alice was ready to go to the Olympics in 1940, but because of World War II, the Olympics were canceled. Alice was ready to go to the Olympics in 1944, but again, because of the war, the Olympics were canceled. In 1948, on a rainy August afternoon in London's Wembley Stadium, Alice cleared 5 feet, 6⅛ inches and won the Olympic gold medal in the high jump, beating out Great Britain's Dorothy Tyler. She was twenty-four years old, nearly six years older than most of her competitors.

When Alice sailed over the bar, she became the first African American woman to win an Olympic gold medal. But when she returned home to Albany, Georgia, for a hero's reception, the local auditorium was segregated, the mayor refused to shake her hand, and she had to exit from the side door.

Still, Alice remained positive. "We had segregation, but it wasn't any problem for me because I had won."

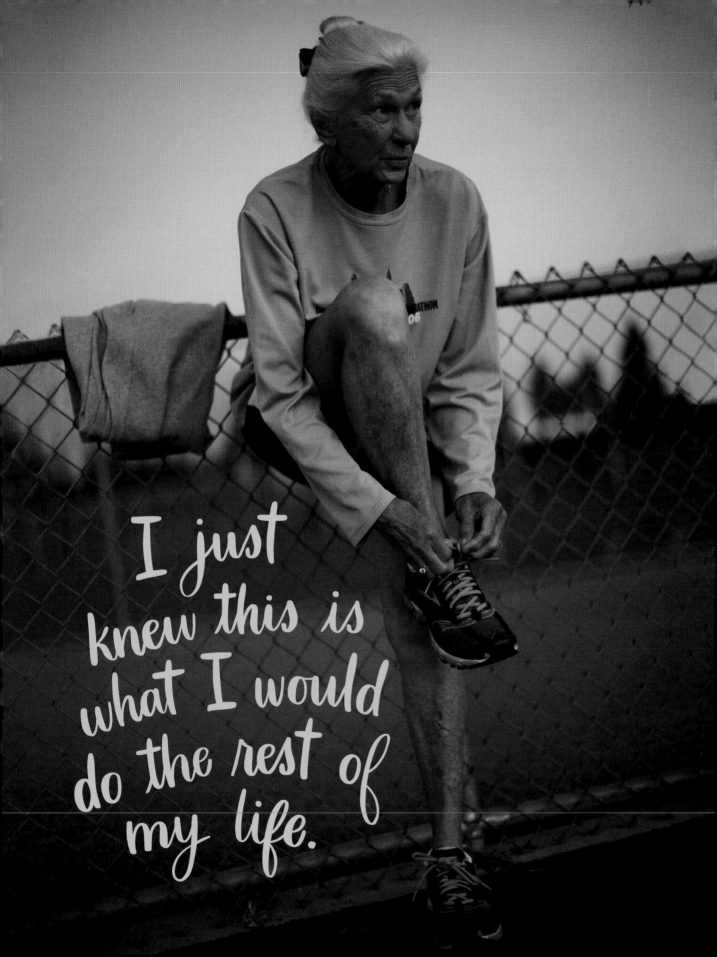

JOY JOHNSON
Marathon Running
DECEMBER 25, 1926–NOVEMBER 4, 2013

WHEN JOY JOHNSON ROSE at four o'clock each morning, before she had her cup of coffee or laced up her sneakers, before she drove to the Willow Glen High school track in San Jose, California, she began the day with Bible verse Isaiah 40:31: "But they who wait for the Lord shall renew their strength; they shall mount up with wings like eagles; they shall run and not be weary; they shall walk and not faint."

Joy had moved to California to escape the frigid midwestern winters of the Minnesota dairy farm where she grew up. She was a high school physical education teacher and track coach, but she never considered herself much of an athlete. That changed when she retired at age fifty-nine. Looking for ways to stay active, Joy began going for walks. But soon walking turned to jogging, one mile, two, and then three. She entered a local road race and then another and another. When her mantel filled with the trophies she won, a friend encouraged her to run the New York City Marathon.

"When I crossed that finish line in Central Park, I just knew this is what I would do the rest of my life," she said. Joy made quilts from her race T-shirts and sent postcards to her granddaughter Leah from New York City each year before she ran.

In 1989, she set the New York City Marathon record for a sixty-two-year-old. Ten years later, she ran her best time of three hours, fifty-five minutes, and thirty seconds. At eighty-one years old, when aging slowed her down and completing a marathon now took nearly seven hours, Joy attended marathon camp and changed her routine by increasing her weekly run totals from thirty to fifty-five miles. She shaved nearly one hour off her marathon time.

At age eighty-six, she promised her daughter that this, her twenty-fifth consecutive New York City Marathon, would be her last. "I'll be at the back of the pack, but I don't mind." At mile twenty, Joy took a fall. Bandaged and bruised, she insisted on continuing the race and limped across the finish line in nearly eight hours. The next afternoon after a TV interview, she returned to her hotel room to nap and never woke up.

Joy's annual postcard to her granddaughter arrived at Leah's dorm dated the day of her death. She died in her running shoes, just as she always wanted.

Winning it once can be a fluke; winning it twice proves you are the best.

ALTHEA GIBSON

Tennis

AUGUST 25, 1927–SEPTEMBER 28, 2003

DANIEL AND ANNIE BELL GIBSON GOT TIRED of scratching out a living as sharecroppers in the cotton fields of Silver, South Carolina, so they packed up their three-year-old daughter, Althea, and headed north to New York City, and a neighborhood called Harlem. Inside their home on 143rd Street, life was just as hard as in the South, but outdoors was altogether different. Baseball, basketball—Althea loved all sports, but in table tennis she couldn't be beat. Long-legged and lightning-fast, Althea became a table tennis champion. When a mentor bought her a racket and invited her to a game of tennis on the Harlem River tennis courts, Althea found a sport she loved even better than all the rest.

Neighbors collected donations to pay for her membership and lessons at Harlem's Cosmopolitan Tennis Club, where one year later she won her first local tournament. Throughout high school and college at Florida A&M, she won every championship in the all-black American Tennis Association events she entered, but her wins didn't earn her any invitations from the white tennis organizations.

That is, until former tennis champion Alice Marble wrote an open letter to *American Lawn Tennis* magazine criticizing the discriminatory practices against Negro tennis players. One month later, Althea received an invitation from the U.S. National Lawn Tennis Association to play in the national championships at Forest Hills. Within two years she was a top ten player. With her strong, athletic style of play, reporters commented, "She hits the ball and plays like a man." By 1953, she ranked number 7. By 1956, she ranked number 2.

She won in France, in Monaco, and in Italy. It was on to the finals. In less than one hour, Althea won the Ladies' Singles Championship in 1957, becoming the first black player to win Wimbledon.

She received a ticker-tape parade, but it was returning to Harlem that reminded her how far she had come. "No matter what accomplishments you make, somebody helped you."

BOBBI GIBB
Marathon Running
b. NOVEMBER 2, 1942

HER FIRST RUNNING PARTNERS WERE DOGS. The neighborhood dogs kept pace with Bobbi Gibb as she made her way through the woods of Winchester, Massachusetts. Each morning, she laced up white leather Red Cross nursing shoes, the only sturdy shoes available for women in the 1960s, and set out. She knew of no other runners and had never seen a track meet, let alone a marathon. But she knew that by herself, outside in the elements, nothing made her quite as happy as running.

After her father took her to see the Boston Marathon, Bobbi, who could log nearly forty miles in one stretch, started thinking about racing. Two years later, from her new home in San Diego, California, she requested an application to compete in the 1966 Boston Marathon. A letter from race officials informed her that women were allowed to run only 1.5 miles competitively. And furthermore, they were "physiologically incapable" of completing a 26.2-mile marathon. That was when Bobbi made up her mind.

She traveled four days aboard a bus headed for Massachusetts. On the morning of the race, Bobbi pulled on a one-piece swimsuit, her brother's Bermuda shorts, a pair of boys' running shoes, and a hooded sweatshirt and made her way to the starting line of the marathon. Patiently, Bobbi waited behind bushes until she heard the starting gun and waited some more until half the pack had passed. And then she jumped in. She was the only runner without a number pinned to her sweatshirt. Several miles in, the runners behind her began to whisper, and she knew they suspected she was a woman. She took off her hood, then peeled off her sweatshirt down to her swimsuit, revealing her figure to the crowd of spectators. Reporters snapped photos, and word quickly spread through the racecourse that a woman was running. By the time she reached the halfway point at Wellesley College, a swell of female students was waiting to cheer her on. She was dehydrated and her feet were blistered, but she kept running. "I knew that I was running for much more than my own personal challenge. I was running to change the way people think." Even with her late start, Bobbi finished with a time of three hours, twenty-one minutes, and forty seconds, in 126th place, ahead of two-thirds of the runners.

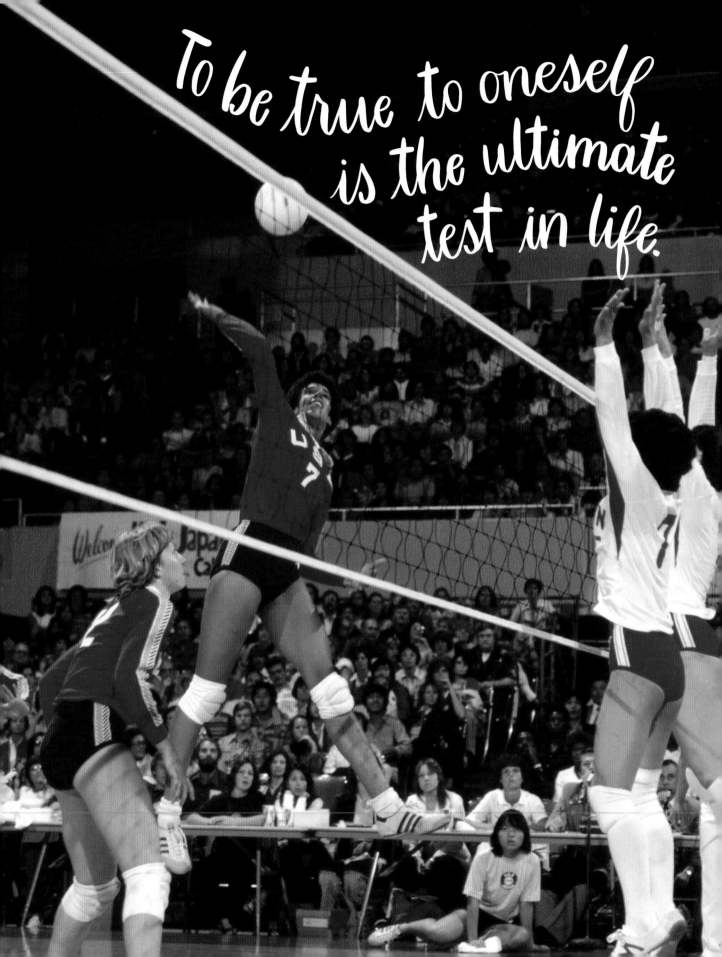

To be true to oneself is the ultimate test in life.

FLO HYMAN
Volleyball
JULY 31, 1954–JANUARY 24, 1986

FLORA JEAN HYMAN WOULD NOT STOP GROWING. She outgrew her clothes, inched past her seven siblings, and sprouted higher than her stately mother. By the time she was twelve years old, she stood eye to eye with her six-foot-tall father. But the more Flo grew, the more she wanted to shrink, especially at her elementary school, where she hunched over to make herself as small as her classmates. Her parents, George and Warrene, demanded that she stand tall. Her height should make her proud, not ashamed, they told her.

On Redondo Beach, not far from her home in Inglewood, California, Flo and her older sister, Suzanne, stood in the crowds, watching the heated beach volleyball matches. It wasn't long before the two joined in the pickup games and tournaments. On the sand, as she sprang up to block shots and spike the ball, Flo found it was the first time in her life she enjoyed being tall.

When Flo reached six feet, five inches tall, she began to stand proud. After the shifting sands of beach volleyball, Flo was well prepared for the indoor courts at Morningside High School and led her volleyball team to victory. The University of Houston offered Flo an athletic scholarship, their first ever given to a female athlete. On the courts, Flo's spin serve soared over the net. Flo's brown skin and Afro stood out in a game played by whites, for whites, but it was her lethal "Flying Clutchman" spike, traveling at a speed of 110 miles per hour, that earned her the collegiate All-American title for three years straight.

In 1980, Flo was selected to be part of the U.S. Olympic team in Moscow, Russia. Though she had to wait four years for her chance at a gold medal when the United States boycotted the games. By the time of the 1984 Olympics in her hometown of Los Angeles, Flo was the oldest member of the team and nicknamed herself the Old Lady. But it was the Old Lady who scored the points needed to win the first-ever U.S. women's volleyball team silver medal in a down-to-the-wire match against the Chinese team.

If you work hard and prepare yourself, you might get beat, but you'll never lose.

NANCY LIEBERMAN
Basketball

b. JULY 1, 1958

AT NIGHT ON THE COURTS OF BROOKLYN, NEW YORK, you couldn't see the basketball, but you could hear it *swish* through the net. They called it radar ball, and Nancy Lieberman could beat every boy she played against. She could beat them in the daylight hours, too—in baseball, softball, and even football.

After Nancy's parents divorced, her mom, Renee, moved her and her brother to Far Rockaway, New York. There Nancy began playing with girls for the first time on her high school basketball team, where she set a school record for assists. Renee didn't mind her daughter playing basketball at school, but when Nancy practiced dribbling in their home, Renee punctured five of her many basketballs with a screwdriver, demanding she practice outdoors.

Nancy went to Montreal, Canada, in 1976 to play on the first U.S. Olympic women's basketball team and, at eighteen years old, became the youngest basketball player in Olympic history to win a silver medal.

Fresh from her Olympic win, Nancy received over one hundred college scholarship offers. She surprised everyone by choosing Old Dominion University in Norfolk, Virginia. "I always wanted to go to a place nobody had heard of because I thought of myself as an underdog, and I wanted to help build something."

She built a winning team as she led Old Dominion to national titles in 1979 and 1980. Fans called her Lady Magic, after famous NBA player Magic Johnson. Both were known for their passing skills, their over-the-top court personality, and the numbers they put on the board. As a sophomore, Nancy achieved an elusive triple-double—double-digit figures in three categories—with forty points, fifteen rebounds, and eleven assists. Nancy left college to go pro and played on a number of teams through 1997, when she joined the Phoenix Mercury in the inaugural year of the WNBA. At fifty years old in 2008, she was the oldest player in the league's history.

After she retired from playing, she became the first woman to coach a professional men's team, the Texas Legends, in 2009.

The only way to escape fear is to trample it beneath your feet.

NADIA COMĂNECI
Gymnastics
b. NOVEMBER 12, 1961

WHEN TWO OF THE COUNTRY'S TOP COACHES went searching for students for their new gymnastics school, they weren't looking for the perfect girl, but they found her in Nadia Comăneci. "Who likes gymnastics?" they asked a group of six-year-olds. Nadia not only raised her hand, she did a flawless cartwheel.

Nadia broke three sofas in four years in her family's home practicing the gymnastic routines she learned in classes. But in that time she also became Romania's national junior champion. In Onești, Romania, where she lived with her parents, Gheorghe and Stefania-Alexandrina, the broken sofas were Nadia's first steps toward making history.

She placed first in an international competition at age twelve, defeating the reigning champion, Olympic gold medalist Ludmilla Tourischeva, to win the European Championships.

By the time she arrived in Montreal, Canada, for the 1976 Olympics, Nadia was being compared to the 1972 Olympic medalist Olga Korbut, the smiling, energetic gymnast from Russia. But Nadia was the opposite of a bubbly gymnast. Her pale, serious face prompted harsh questions from reporters about her happiness. While Olga came to smile, Nadia pointed out, "I want to win a gold medal."

On the first night of competition, fourteen-year-old Nadia scored a 9.9 on the beam and then moved on to the uneven bars. She stunned the crowd with her grace as she glided from bar to bar, completed a flawless handstand, and landed a flying dismount. The crowds were stunned again when the judges scored Nadia just a 1.00 out of a possible 10. Her coach ran to the judges' table to demand an answer. The problem wasn't with Nadia's routine, they explained. The problem was with the scoreboard. It wasn't designed to register a four-digit score of 10.00, so they were forced to display a 1.00 to represent Nadia's perfect 10, an Olympic gymnastics first. The crowd roared, and Nadia's once-solemn face broke into a smile, her first of the competition.

She kept smiling the next night when she scored 10.00 again on the balance beam, floor exercises, and uneven bars. But by now, the crowd knew that when the scoreboard read 1.00, with Nadia, it meant perfect.

DIANA GOLDEN

Skiing

MARCH 20, 1963–AUGUST 25, 2001

IT'S DIFFICULT ENOUGH TO SKI ON TWO LEGS, but Diana Golden did it on one. Diana began life as an active girl who loved to ski the New Hampshire slopes of Cannon Mountain. At age twelve, while she was returning from her daily run, her leg collapsed, and Diana was rushed to the hospital. Bone cancer, the doctors told her family. Diana had just one question: "Can I ski again?"

Six months later, after her right leg was amputated at the knee, Diana was fitted with a prosthetic leg and had to learn again how to walk. Working with a ski instructor from the New England Handicapped Ski Association, she also learned to ski using outriggers, crutches with small skis attached. In high school, Diana joined the Lincoln-Sudbury ski team, and at seventeen years old, joined the U.S. Disabled Ski Team, where she won gold in the downhill and silver in the giant slalom in her first races.

At Dartmouth College in New Hampshire, she continued skiing and, during the off-season, built her leg strength on dry land by racing around the track on crutches, hopping stadium steps at Alumni Field, and attending racing academies. With her successes came questions about her future, and Diana made the decision to leave skiing for good, or so she thought. It would take nearly three years before her passion for skiing returned. But when it did, it took only one year before she again began blazing a trail on the slopes, winning medals in every competition she entered and a spot on the 1988 Olympic team in Calgary, Canada.

Adaptive skiing was first introduced as a demonstration sport during the 1988 Olympic Games, and it was Diana who led the U.S. team to a medal sweep, winning gold, silver, and bronze in the women's disabled giant slalom. Attempting to reach greater speeds during competitions, Diana exchanged her outriggers in 1990 for standard ski poles and improved her downhill time to sixty-five miles per hour.

Because of Diana's advocacy, in 1985, the U.S. Ski and Snowboard Association began allowing disabled skiers to race as early seeds in able-bodied events, providing safer race conditions, and called the new safeguards the Golden Rule.

"I'm not out there because I'm brave and courageous. I'm out there because I want to go fast, and I want to win."

True champions aren't always the ones who win but those with the most guts.

I want to make it big and make it better than last time.

MIA HAMM
Soccer
b. MARCH 17, 1972

EVEN THOUGH SHE WAS NICKNAMED for the famous ballerina Mia Slavenska, Mariel Margaret Hamm preferred playing soccer and football over performing pliés and pirouettes.

Born with a clubfoot, Mia chased down soccer balls in her backyard in her corrective shoes from the time she was a toddler. Tagging along behind her eight-year-old brother, Garrett, five-year-old Mia was one of the first he picked for his touch football team because of her quick hands and lightning speed.

Mia's father was an air force colonel, so she and her five siblings traveled from town to town, base to base, with their parents. From Virginia to Texas to Alabama to Florence, Italy, Mia picked up skills in each of the places she lived. She joined the boys' football team as a split end and defensive back in junior high school, but when she got to Notre Dame High School in Wichita Falls, Texas, she became a forward on the soccer team. Mia focused on being a team player, never once scoring a goal during her first year. But during her second, Anson Dorrance, a coach at the University of North Carolina, was visiting a tournament in Louisiana. When he couldn't take his eyes off one of the Texas players because of her speed and athleticism, he knew instantly that she was the girl he'd heard so much about. "Is that Mia Hamm?" he asked.

The next year, he invited her to play with the women's national soccer team. At fifteen years old, she was the youngest player in the team's history.

Mia led the Tar Heels soccer team at the University of North Carolina to four NCAA championships, scoring 103 goals. For Mia, it was the dedication to the sport that separated good players from great ones. She often completed extra workouts alone in the park, running cones and sprints. When a coach told her she ran like a girl, she told him that if he ran a little faster, he could, too.

Though she was a gifted striker, her speed, footwork, and passing skills allowed her to play as a forward, or at any offensive position she was needed.

In 1991, FIFA formed the very first Women's World Cup soccer tournament in China, and Mia became their youngest player, at age nineteen. Her goals helped the U.S. team advance and win the first World Cup trophy awarded.

Winning never gets old.

LISA LESLIE
Basketball
b. JULY 7, 1972

BORN IN GARDENA, CALIFORNIA, Lisa Leslie heard the same question nearly every day of her life: "Do you play basketball?" And she answered with the same response nearly every day of her life: "No." Being a six-foot, two-inch-tall twelve-year-old meant people assumed she would play.

Her mom, Christine, raised Lisa and her sisters on her own, working first as a mail carrier and then as a long-haul trucker. She told her daughters they were descendants of African royalty and enrolled them in charm school, where Lisa improved her posture by balancing books on her head. But Lisa still didn't want to be told she had to play a sport just because she was tall. To stop the questions, she decided to play one game: a pickup game in her neighborhood. Lisa played center and simply had to hold up her arms to block the other players' shots. Once Lisa started playing, she never wanted to stop.

She competed against other girls for the first time when she tried out for the Whaley Junior High School team. Her cousin Craig, a high school basketball player, told her she'd need more than just height; she'd need strength, stamina, and skill. For months she trained with Craig, doing sit-ups and push-ups and jumping rope. He taught her hook shots, dribbling, and passing. In her sophomore year of high school, she began receiving mail and calls daily from colleges wanting her to join their teams.

Lisa bounded into the air for three-point jumpers—and cheers—as she became the very first high school girl to slam-dunk. In one game at the end of her senior year, Lisa alone scored 102 points in the first half. She would have beaten the game total record of 106 points if the other team hadn't refused to come out of the locker room after halftime.

Lisa set her sights on the Olympics and the Atlanta Games in 1996, earning gold with her team. When the NBA kicked off its women's league, the WNBA, Lisa was one of the first players recruited. On the Los Angeles Sparks, number 9 helped to bring national attention to the league by once again being the first woman to slam-dunk during a professional game. Lisa returned to the Olympics in 2000, 2004, and 2008, winning gold each time.

VENUS AND SERENA WILLIAMS

Tennis

b. JUNE 17, 1980, AND SEPTEMBER 26, 1981

BY THE TIME THEY COULD WALK, Venus and Serena Williams were holding tennis rackets. It was their father Richard's dream to have two tennis-champion daughters. So, before they were born, he studied the sport and taught himself and his wife, Oracene, to play, and they in turn taught their daughters. Nearly every day of the week, Richard drove them to the local courts in their Compton neighborhood of Los Angeles, which were littered with trash and strung with chain-link nets. When shots rang out from rival-gang gunfire, their father reminded the girls to focus on their game. "Never mind the noise," he told them. "Just play."

And play they did. By age four, Venus could hit five hundred tennis balls during practice. By age ten, she had sixty-three tournament wins and was ranked number 1 in her age group. Not far behind was her little sister, Serena. Richard made up practices where they hit tennis balls so deflated, they barely bounced. They warmed up by throwing rackets in the air, took karate and ballet lessons to gain discipline and agility, and caught footballs to improve their hand-eye coordination.

Their father knew that two young black girls would encounter fierce racism in the nearly all-white sport, so he paid busloads of onlookers to taunt the girls as they practiced to prepare them for what they might hear at tennis matches on the professional circuit. If they could play through this, they could play through anything, he reasoned.

They moved to Florida to begin training with coach Rick Macci, and at fourteen years old, Venus turned professional. The next year, Serena joined her. By sixteen and seventeen, they were both ranked in the top fifty.

Venus and Serena were criticized for expressing emotion on the court, for their father touting their wins, for sporting beads in their hair, and for wearing decorative tennis outfits. They were criticized for being black. But together in doubles or apart in singles, when the Williams sisters took to the court, the stands were packed.

As they traveled the world to compete in tournaments, they stayed together in hotels, sharing a room as they had as young girls in Los Angeles. The crowds kept coming to see the two sisters defeat every top-ranked player until they reached numbers 1 and 2 following the French Open in 2002.

It's important to me that youth everywhere, no matter their race, religion, or gender, know that anything is possible with perseverance.

IBTIHAJ MUHAMMAD
Fencing
b. DECEMBER 4, 1985

IN OLYMPIC VILLAGE, she became known as "the girl in the scarf." But Ibtihaj Muhammad was so much more than a girl in a scarf. She was the very first Muslim American to wear a hijab while competing for the U.S. Olympic team.

Her father, Eugene, and mother, Denise, converted to Islam and raised all of their five children in the Muslim faith. They required each of their children to participate in sports as a possible means to college scholarships, but it fell to Denise to customize sports uniforms to make sure her daughters' arms and legs were covered when they participated in tennis, softball, track and field, volleyball, and swimming. One day, when she and thirteen-year-old Ibti drove past a high school in their Maplewood, New Jersey, neighborhood, they watched students practicing a sport covered from head to toe in bodysuits and helmets.

"I didn't know what it was, but I saw how they were dressed," Denise said. When Ibti entered Columbia High School, she joined the fencing team.

Fencing to Ibti was much like the sword fighting she and her brother did with sticks in their backyard, and soon she led her high school team to two state championships. In school, she, her siblings, and several Muslim classmates were often teased and ostracized because of their religion, but Ibti remained focused on her goal of competing and in 2003 was awarded a fencing scholarship to Duke University. Unfortunately, following her many wins and her three NCAA titles, an injury prevented her from making the fencing team for the 2012 Olympics. However, after Ibti healed, she refocused her efforts on competing in 2016.

As a devout Muslim, she prayed five times a day, but in between prayers she trained hard by running, working out with her personal trainer, practicing footwork and technique, and sparring for one hour at the end of each day. She arrived at the 2016 Olympics in Rio as one of many athletes from around the world, but she left as the first Muslim American Olympic medal winner when she won bronze for fencing in the team sabre. Fans flocked to the girl in the hijab for autographs. Fellow Olympian Carmelo Anthony, one of her many fans, told her, "You're changing lives all over the world."

I do not dwell
on what could have been.
Instead, I look to what can be.

TATYANA McFADDEN
Track and Field
b. APRIL 21, 1989

NOTHING COULD SLOW DOWN six-year-old Tatyana. Not even spina bifida, a condition from birth that paralyzed her legs. When her Russian orphanage couldn't afford a wheelchair, Tatyana used only her hands to speed-walk across the floors.

On a trip to the orphanage, Deborah McFadden, visiting for her work with the U.S. Health Department, immediately noticed the bright-eyed bundle of energy.

"That's my mom," Tatyana told the orphanage director.

When the two returned to Baltimore, Maryland, as mother and daughter, doctors informed Deborah that Tatyana, who was underfed and had received no medical care in the orphanage, likely wouldn't survive. Deborah responded by contacting Gerry Herman, a coach, trainer, and advocate at the Kennedy Krieger Institute who worked with children with disabilities, to help Tatyana build her strength with swimming, gymnastics, and even scuba diving.

Deborah didn't speak much Russian, but she quickly learned Tatyana's favorite phrase, "*Ya sama.*" I can do it myself.

Tatyana grew stronger each year. At age eight, she was fitted with a racing wheelchair. At nine, she decided she wanted to become a professional athlete. At fifteen years old, she became the youngest athlete in the Summer Paralympics in Athens, Greece.

She returned home with a silver medal in the 100-meter and a bronze in the 200, but back at Atholton High School, Tatyana's track team refused to let her race alongside able-bodied racers, requiring Tatyana to circle the track by herself, a lone blur in her wheelchair.

When her coach at the University of Illinois, also a wheelchair racer, suggested she try longer distances, Tatyana agreed to enter the Chicago Marathon in 2009. After winning, she was asked by reporters how a sprinter became a marathoner, and Tatyana replied, "Well, I just love doing the four hundred meters. So I told myself I was just doing it one hundred times."

In 2013, she added wins in the Boston, London, and New York City marathons to become the only person to win every major marathon in the same year, setting new course records in two of them. She won all four again in the next three years.

Tatyana inspired a nation of athletes, including her adopted younger sisters, Ruthi and Hannah, both of whom have disabilities. Hannah competed alongside her sister at the 2012 Paralympics.

GABBY DOUGLAS
Gymnastics
b. DECEMBER 31, 1995

IT ALL STARTED WITH A CARTWHEEL. A one-handed cartwheel. When Arielle Hawkins showed her youngest sister the cartwheel she learned in gymnastics class, three-year-old Gabby knew immediately she wanted to be a gymnast. Her mother, Natalie, wasn't so sure. But after three years of Gabby's begging, and climbing the furniture, Natalie signed her up for lessons. Two years later, at age eight, Gabby became the Virginia state gymnastics champion.

Gabrielle Christina Victoria Douglas was a big name for a small girl. At birth, Gabby was diagnosed with a rare blood disorder, making it difficult for her to eat. Gabby eventually outgrew her condition but never grew beyond four feet, eleven inches.

From Excalibur, the gym where Gabby trained, she quickly advanced to the highest level in gymnastics. And after watching Shawn Johnson win gold in the 2008 Olympics, Gabby decided that she would compete in 2012. But first, she decided, she needed to train with Shawn's gymnastics coach, Liang Chow. The only problem was, she lived in Virginia Beach, Virginia, and he lived nearly fifteen hundred miles away in Des Moines, Iowa. Again, Gabby begged her mother, and again, her mother said no. Gabby kept competing, and when she won first place at the Pan American Championships, her mother agreed to let her train in Iowa. Staying with a host family, the Partons, Gabby began her training with Liang Chow. When she got homesick or yearned for the life of a normal teenager, it was her mother who reminded her, "You have to fight, and just refuse to quit."

Gabby not only refused to quit, she trained six days a week on the uneven bars, floor exercises, balance beam, and vault. In June 2012, Gabby received the highest score at the Olympic Trials and earned the top spot on the 2012 Olympic team. She smiled so big and flew so high when performing her uneven bars routine, she was called "the Flying Squirrel."

From the stands, her family sat alongside the Partons and watched as Gabby made history as the first African American gymnast to become the Olympic individual all-around champion and the first American gymnast to win gold in the individual all-around and team competitions at the same Olympic Games.

When I was swimming for my life, I never would have believed I would be where I am now.

YUSRA MARDINI
Swimming
b. MARCH 5, 1998

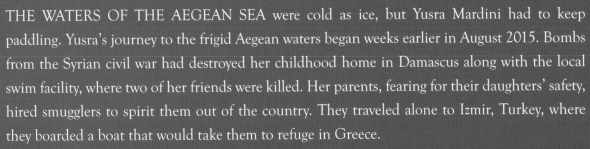

THE WATERS OF THE AEGEAN SEA were cold as ice, but Yusra Mardini had to keep paddling. Yusra's journey to the frigid Aegean waters began weeks earlier in August 2015. Bombs from the Syrian civil war had destroyed her childhood home in Damascus along with the local swim facility, where two of her friends were killed. Her parents, fearing for their daughters' safety, hired smugglers to spirit them out of the country. They traveled alone to Izmir, Turkey, where they boarded a boat that would take them to refuge in Greece.

For three hours, Yusra and her sister, Sarah, held up their small dinghy, designed for six and filled with eighteen migrants, as it began taking on water when the motor stopped working. They first threw luggage overboard, but when the boat continued to sink, the sisters, two of only three swimmers on board, jumped in to hold up the boat, kicking so hard to stay afloat, they lost their shoes. In the dark of night, Yusra's arms were tired and her eyes stung from the ocean's salt water, but the scared faces of the other refugees kept her pushing onward. When they reached the island of Lesbos hours later, her journey continued on land until they reached a refugee shelter in Berlin, Germany.

A translator at the shelter discovered Yusra had been trained as a swimmer by her father, a coach, since age three and introduced her to the German swim coach Sven Spannekrebs.

"She's a really tough athlete," Coach Spannekrebs noted, impressed by her work ethic. Tough enough, he thought, to begin training for the 2020 Olympics in Japan. Six hours a day, in a pool built by Nazis for the 1936 Berlin Olympics, Yusra swam laps and built her endurance. When they received word that the International Olympic Committee was looking to start a refugee team, Yusra tried out and made the 2016 team, four years ahead of schedule.

Yusra and nine other athletes, who also fled their homes in the war-torn countries of Ethiopia, South Sudan, and the Democratic Republic of the Congo, entered Maracanã Stadium in Rio de Janeiro behind the host team. Marching to the Olympic Anthem, the team proudly waved as the crowd rose to applaud the first-ever Refugee Olympic Team.

MO'NE DAVIS
Baseball
b. JUNE 24, 2001

BEFORE SHE ENTERED THE NINTH GRADE, Mo'ne Davis was already the most popular girl in high school. Being featured on the cover of the August 2014 issue of *Sports Illustrated* has a way of making a girl stand out. As the only girl to ever pitch a shutout and the first African American girl to play in the Little League World Series, Mo'ne was used to standing out.

She began playing basketball at age five with her brother Qu'ran, who chose his little sister for pickup games. As a point guard, she made up for her petite size with her speed and a competitive streak. Once, in a fierce one-on-one battle with her brother, she won in an upset after trailing by several points. Her mom wasn't thrilled with her only daughter playing sports with boys. She tried dressing Mo'ne up and fussing over her hair, but Mo'ne preferred balls to dolls. When Mo'ne insisted on trying out for the basketball team, her mom gave in and gave up.

Basketball led her to football, and football led her to baseball, when Steve Bandura, a program director at her South Philadelphia rec center, first noticed that eight-year-old Mo'ne could throw a perfect spiral. He soon discovered there wasn't a sport Mo'ne couldn't master. He tried her out as a pitcher for his baseball team, the Philadelphia Taney Dragons.

Mo'ne's fast sidearm delivery led to an 8–0 shutout over a team from Newark, New Jersey, and it helped her team advance to the Mid-Atlantic region of the Little League World Series. There, her seventy-mile-per-hour pitching struck out eight hitters on the Nashville team. By the fifth inning, Mo'ne had given up only two infield hits. While the Nashville pitcher reached his eighty-five-pitch limit, Mo'ne had just forty-four. She only needed a few more pitches to strike out the side in the final inning to win the Little League World Series title for her team.

AFTER THE WHISTLE

CONSTANCE APPLEBEE

In 1981, the NCAA accepted field hockey as an official college sport. That year, Constance passed away at 107 years old, just a few months before the first NCAA Field Hockey championship game was played.

LIZZIE ARLINGTON

Born Elizabeth Stride (or Stroud), Lizzie paved the way for many female baseball pitchers, including Alta Weiss, Lizzie Murphy, and Jackie Mitchell, during the early years of baseball.

ETHELDA BLEIBTREY

In 1928, Ethelda was again jailed for swimming "nude" without stockings, in the Central Park reservoir in New York City. Publicity surrounding the event raised awareness about women's restrictive swimwear. New York City mayor Jimmy Walker intervened on her behalf, and as a result of Ethelda's stunt, New York City built its very first public swimming pool.

MILDRED ELLA "BABE" DIDRIKSON ZAHARIAS

Called Terrific Tomboy, the Texas Tornado, Superman's Sister, Mrs. Golf, and the Greatest Woman Athlete in the World, Babe was a founding member of the LPGA in 1947 and was inducted into the Hall of Fame of Women's Golf in 1951. She was the second-oldest woman to win an LPGA tournament. Babe was named the tenth greatest U.S. athlete by ESPN and has been featured on a U.S. postage stamp. A controversial figure, Babe was known to hold racist and anti-Semitic views . . . even as she forged new paths for women in sports.

ALICE COACHMAN

Alice Coachman's winning Olympic jump set a new world record that stood until 1956. In 1932, Louise Stokes and Tidye Pickett became the first African American women to qualify for the Olympics; however, due to discrimination, they were not allowed to compete. In 1936, they were on the Olympic team again, but Stokes was sidelined and Pickett—officially the first

African American woman to compete in the Olympics—broke her foot on a hurdle and did not complete her event.

JOY JOHNSON

Joy completed twenty-five consecutive marathons, beginning at age sixty-two, and placed first in her age group for five of them.

ALTHEA GIBSON

Althea was also the first black person to win a Grand Slam title and the U.S. Nationals and to compete in a U.S. National Championship and on a pro tour. She earned a total of fifty-six singles and doubles championships before turning pro in 1959. She retired in 1971 and was inducted into the International Tennis Hall of Fame. "I have all the opportunities today because of people like Althea," Venus Williams said. "Just trying to follow in her footsteps."

BOBBI GIBB

In 1972, six years after Bobbi's first appearance in the marathon, the Amateur Athletic Union changed the rules to allow women to compete in marathons. In 1996, Bobbi Gibb's name was added to the list of winners inscribed on the Boston Marathon memorial in Copley Square. At seventy-three, she was the grand marshal of the 2016 Boston Marathon, commemorating the fiftieth anniversary of her first run.

FLO HYMAN

Flo was credited with highlighting women's volleyball and making the sport more appealing to women of color. During a match in Japan in 1986, she collapsed and died due to Marfan syndrome, a genetic disorder. In 1987, the Women's Sports Foundation established the Flo Hyman Memorial Award for athletes who exemplified her "dignity, spirit, and commitment to excellence." Diana Golden, Nadia Comăneci, and Lisa Leslie were all winners of this award.

NANCY LIEBERMAN

Working for the Sacramento Kings in 2015, Nancy became the second female assistant coach in NBA history. In 2018, she was named head coach of the BIG3 team Power, becoming the first-ever female head coach of a men's professional team.

NADIA COMĂNECI

Nadia became the youngest Olympic gymnast all-around champion, a record she holds to this day. In the 1976 Olympics, Nadia earned three gold medals and seven perfect 10s. The Comăneci Salto, an uneven bars somersault maneuver, is named in her honor.

DIANA GOLDEN

After retirement in 1990, Diana became a motivational speaker and an avid rock climber, successfully scaling Mount Rainier. Following her death from cancer at age thirty-eight, Disabled Sports USA established the Diana Golden Race Series.

MIA HAMM

In 1996, Mia competed on the first women's soccer team at the Olympic Games in Atlanta and returned in 2000 and 2004, where she was the first soccer player to carry the American flag during opening ceremonies. She earned two Olympic gold medals. Up until 2013, she held the record for the most international goals scored by a woman or a man. She was named to the FIFA 100 list of the greatest living soccer players.

LISA LESLIE

Lisa was a co-owner of the WNBA team the Los Angeles Sparks from 2011 to 2013. She played for the Sparks for eleven seasons, through 2009. In 2015, she was inducted into the Basketball Hall of Fame.

VENUS AND SERENA WILLIAMS

In 2000, Venus became the first African American to win Wimbledon since Althea Gibson in 1957. In 1999, Serena became the first African American to win the U.S. Open since Althea in 1958. Combined, the sisters have won twelve Wimbledon singles titles, four Olympic gold medals, and titles in the Australian Open and the French Open.

IBTIHAJ MUHAMMAD

As of 2018, Ibtihaj was a sports ambassador serving on the U.S. Department of State's Empowering Women and Girls through Sports Initiative.

TATYANA McFADDEN

Tatyana and her mother filed and won a lawsuit against the Maryland school district, which led to the passage of a new law requiring Maryland schools to allow athletes with disabilities to compete in school sports.

GABBY DOUGLAS

In 2016, Gabby returned to the Olympics and helped her team win their second consecutive Olympic gold medal.

YUSRA MARDINI

Yusra failed to qualify for the semifinals in the 2016 Olympics, but she said of her experience, "In the water, there is no difference if you are a refugee or a Syrian or German." In 2017, Yusra was appointed the youngest-ever goodwill ambassador for the refugee agency UNHCR. As of 2018, she was looking forward to earning Olympic gold in the 2020 Olympics.

MO'NE DAVIS

In 1972, Maria Pepe was the first girl to earn a spot in the Little League World Series. When she took to the field and the other teams objected, she was removed from the game. The National Organization for Women sued the league on her behalf, and in 1973 Judge Sylvia Pressler ruled against the league. This landmark ruling allowed girls to play in the league beginning in 1974. Forty years later, Mo'ne became the eighteenth girl, out of nearly nine thousand participants, to play in a Little League World Series. She was the fifth female pitcher in World Series history.